MUDFLOWS AND LANDSLIDES

MICHAEL WOODS AND MARY B WOODS

LERNER BOOKS • MINNEAPOLIS

D0412923

To Cathleen Woods

Editor's note: Determining the exact death toll following disasters is often difficult – if not impossible – especially in the case of disasters that took place long ago. The authors and the editors in this series have used their best judgement in determining which figures to include.

First published in the United Kingdom in 2010 by
Lerner Books,
Dalton House,
60 Windsor Avenue,
London SW19 2RR

Website address: www.lernerbooks.co.uk

This edition was updated and edited for UK publication by Discovery Books Ltd.,
First Floor, 2 College Street, Ludlow, Shropshire SY8 1AN

British Library Cataloguing in Publication Data
  Woods, Michael, 1943-
  Mudflows and landslides. - 2nd ed. - (Disasters up close)
  1. Landslides - Juvenile literature
  I. Title II. Woods, Mary B. (Mary Boyle), 1946-
  363.3'492

ISBN-13: 978 0 7613 4408 7

Printed in China

Contents

INTRODUCTION 4

What Are Mudflows and Landslides? 6

What Causes Mudflows and Landslides? 14

Mudflow and Landslide Country 24

Measuring Mudflows and Landslides 30

People Helping People 40

The Future 50

TIMELINE 56

GLOSSARY 58

PLACES TO VISIT 58

SOURCE NOTES 59

SELECTED BIBLIOGRAPHY 60

FURTHER RESOURCES 61

INDEX 62

Introduction

WEIRD NOISES WOKE JUAN TACAXOY. IT WAS THE 5 OCTOBER 2005. TACAXOY LIVED IN PANABAJ, A VILLAGE IN THE CENTRAL AMERICAN COUNTRY OF GUATEMALA.

Tacaxoy went outside and saw a 2-metre deep river of mud flowing towards his home. 'About 10 minutes later came the water and sand,' Tacaxoy said, 'and a little later the rocks and tree trunks.'

Mud and debris fill the area where the Guatemalan villages of Zanchaj and Panabaj used to be. Heavy rains from Hurricane Stan caused mudflows throughout Central America in October 2005.

Tacaxoy and all 30 members of his family lived through the mudflow. Other people in Central America and southern Mexico were not so lucky. Mudflows were happening all over the area. The mud was swallowing people alive. 'The problem was it was in the middle of the night; everyone was sleeping,' said Dr Francisco Mendes Beauc, who had come from a nearby village to help the survivors.

Four days of heavy rain from Hurricane Stan had soaked the ground. Rain had turned the soil into thick mud. Sheets of mud on the sides of mountains and hills began to flow downwards. Rivers of mud up to 12 m thick poured over houses and other buildings.

Mud is heavy enough to crush buildings and carry away cars. Mud just a few centimetres deep can trap people. People buried under the mud may suffocate (die from lack of air to breathe). People may also become ill from swallowing mud and breathing it into their noses.

As the mud flowed over the ground, it picked up tree branches, broken glass and rocks the size of footballs. Those objects scraped against people, animals and buildings.

Alexander Flores's home in San Salvador, the capital of El Salvador, was buried under 2 m of mud. His mother and five of his brothers and sisters died. 'I just heard two shouts from my mother, saying 'Alex, Alex,' maybe for me to help her or her trying to save me.'

Deep mud covered roads and made it hard for rescue workers to arrive and help. In Panabaj, mud covered the roofs of buildings. Rescue workers could not even find homes where people might be buried.

'We are asking that [Panabaj] be declared a cemetery,' said Diego Esquina, the mayor of Panabaj. 'We are tired, [and] we no longer know where to dig.' He said that 1,000 to 1,500 people were probably buried beneath the mud.

Nobody knows how many people died after Hurricane Stan because many bodies could not be found. The mudflows killed at least 750 people, injured hundreds of others, and destroyed about 100,000 people's homes.

El Salvador also experienced Hurricane Stan. That same week, the volcano Ilamatepec erupted and sent streams of hot mud, called lahars, down the mountainside.

I was like a worm sliding around in the mud.

– Alexander Flores, whose home in El Salvador was buried by a mudflow in 2005

What Are Mudflows and Landslides?

MUDFLOWS ARE WET EARTH THAT FLOWS DOWN THE SIDES OF MOUNTAINS OR HILLS. THE MUD IS THICK, ALMOST LIKE TOOTHPASTE. IT IS MADE UP OF SOIL, STONES AND OTHER MATERIAL MIXED WITH WATER FROM RAIN OR MELTED SNOW.

Mudflows may be more than 200 m wide and 9 m deep. Some whoosh along at more than 50 kph (30 mph). They can go great distances, too. In 1877 a mudflow in Ecuador travelled more than 310 km (192 miles).

A mudflow usually gets bigger as it moves along. The flow grows by scooping up trees, soil and rocks. Mudflows can carry away people, animals, houses, cars, bridges and other things in their path.

LANDSLIDES

Landslides are masses of soil and rock that break loose from hills and mountains and slide down. Some landslides involve only a few rocks. In others, the whole side of a

FAST FACT: SLUMPS

Slumps *(below)* are landslides with nowhere to go. In a slump, a large amount of soil, rock or other material drops downwards, but it moves only a short distance, then piles up and stops. Slumps happen when material drops onto flat land, rather than a hillside.

In 2006 a landslide ripped apart this hillside in the Philippines.

mountain breaks off. As the dirt and rocks tumble downwards, they destroy anything in their way. Landslides can easily destroy entire buildings.

The material in a landslide may be wet, but it does not become a thick liquid. Landslides do not usually travel far. A landslide may move only 30–60 m.

Landslides can happen suddenly, killing people and destroying property without warning. Others happen very slowly. Part of a hill may slip only 2.5 centimetres in 100 years.

A covered road is being built to protect drivers from the frequent landslides in this part of northern Italy.

ONE DISASTER LEADS TO ANOTHER

Mudflows and landslides can cause terrible disasters. Disasters are events involving great destruction. Mudflows and landslides damage buildings, underground pipes, electric wires and other property.

Landslides in the UK are mostly very small, and often only cause minimal damage.

CREEPY GRAVESTONES

Have you ever seen old gravestones in a cemetery? Did any of them lean downhill? If so, creep probably tilted them. Creep is a very slow movement of the ground. The soil may move only 0.25 cm each year. Although it takes many years, creep can tilt gravestones, fences, trees and other objects in the ground.

Heavy rains loosened a cemetery-packed hillside above the town of Teziutlán in south-central Mexico. The massive mudflow in 1999 buried as many as 200 people.

However, big landslides such as that which happened in Aberfan in Wales caused many deaths and a great deal of damage.

In the rest of the world, these disasters may cause thousands of deaths and injuries each year. They may cause many billions of dollars worth of damage.

Mudflows and landslides can set the stage for other disasters. Landslides that block rivers can cause floods. Landslides on the ocean floor can cause tsunamis. These monster waves can crash down on the shore, causing great damage. In 1998 an undersea landslide caused a tsunami that killed thousands of people in Papua New Guinea.

In 1998 a tsunami destroyed several villages in northern Papua New Guinea.

In California's Sierra Nevada range, in the USA, a landslide fans out towards Lake Tahoe. The massive landslide closed Highway 89 for 18 months.

Scientists removed the mud that buried the Roman town of Herculaneum nearly 2,000 years ago.

AD 79
HERCULANEUM

About 5,000 people lived in Herculaneum. That beautiful seaside town was in the modern country of Italy. People went there to escape the hot, noisy cities. They enjoyed the bright sun and blue water of the Bay of Naples.

Herculaneum is located at the foot of Mount Vesuvius. This mountain is a volcano – an opening in the Earth's surface that sometimes erupts. During an eruption, smoke, ash (tiny pieces of rock) and hot gases come out of the volcano. Melted rock and mud may flow down the volcano's sides.

On 24 August AD 79, Mount Vesuvius erupted. This eruption is famous for burying the nearby city of Pompeii in ash. It also buried Herculaneum in mud. Steam or liquid water was released during the eruption. It mixed with black, sandy ash that had been deposited on Vesuvius's sides during earlier eruptions and became mud.

A student named Pliny the Younger watched the eruption. He was staying with his mother and his uncle about 32 km (20 miles) away, in the town of Misenum.

'[A] fearful black cloud . . . parted to reveal great tongues of fire . . . ,' Pliny wrote. **'[D]arkness fell . . . as if the lamp had been put out in a closed room.'**

Vesuvius began to erupt shortly after noon. At first people in Herculaneum probably just stayed in their homes. By late afternoon, the eruption became worse. People probably started to flee.

Nobody knows what it was like in Herculaneum as people tried to escape from the disaster. Pliny saw terrible scenes nearby in Misenum. **'[S]ome were calling their parents'**, he wrote, **'others their children or their wives. . . . [S]ome . . . prayed for death in their terror of dying.'**

It may have been hard for people to escape from Herculaneum. Mud often flows faster than people can run. It can as fast as 53 kph (33 mph). Herculaneum was buried under mud up to 23 m thick. The town remained lost to the world for almost 1,800 years. In 1709 people digging a well

' You could hear
the shrieks of women,
the wailing of infants,
and the shouting of men. '

– Pliny the Younger, who witnessed the eruption of Italy's Mount Vesuvius in AD 79

rediscovered it. We know that at least 332 people died in the mudflow. Scientists have found those bodies preserved in the hardened mud.

Mud coated buildings, statues, tools and other things in the town. The mud preserved these objects. When scientists removed the mud, they saw what life was like 2,000 years ago.

Archaeologists have uncovered human skeletons in Herculaneum. The volcanic mudflow killed residents instantly.

What Causes Mudflows and Landslides?

MUDFLOWS AND LANDSLIDES BOTH HAPPEN BECAUSE OF A FORCE — SOMETHING THAT PUSHES OR PULLS ON OBJECTS. THAT FORCE IS GRAVITY. GRAVITY PULLS OBJECTS TOWARDS THE THE EARTH'S CENTRE. IT HOLDS PLATES ON THE DINNER TABLE. IT STOPS PEOPLE FROM FLOATING IN THE AIR.

In the same way, gravity pulls on stones and soil on the sides of hills or mountains. Those objects usually don't tumble down because they have inertia. Inertia makes still objects stay still. It makes objects in motion keep moving.

Rocks and soil also stay in place because of friction. Friction is a force that makes it more difficult for one object to slide against another. Gravity alone isn't strong enough to overcome friction and make objects move, it needs a helping hand.

GIVING GRAVITY A HAND

Rain or melting snow often causes landslides. Water soaking into soil makes it heavier. About 5 cm of rain adds almost 23,000 kilograms of water to a 15 m by 31 m area of soil.

HEAVY MUD

Mud can suck the shoes and socks off your feet because it is so heavy. Just 4 litres of water weigh 4 kg. Mud can be more than twice as heavy as water. That's because it is water with dirt and stones added. That weight crushes buildings caught in mudflows. It also presses on people and makes it difficult for them to escape.

In Indonesia, homeowners try to move through heavy mud following a mudflow in 2006.

'After four or five days [of rain], you could have 113 tonnes of water, and that water's got to go somewhere,' said Tom Horning, a geologist. Water helps soil to overcome friction and become slippery. Water-soaked soil can slide more easily than dry soil.

Certain kinds of soil and rock slip easily. Loose soil that lies on top of solid rock is very dangerous. Rain can soak the soil, but it cannot drain away through the rock. The soil gets heavier and heavier. Just as water on a floor can make a person slip, water can make the soil slip over the underlying rock.

Loose clay is dangerous too. In 1971 heavy rain soaked a layer of loose clay and sand around the village of Saint-Jean-Vianney in Quebec, Canada. A river of mud flowed into the village. It buried 31 people and destroyed 40 homes.

DID YOU KNOW?

Geologists are the scientists who study mudflows and landslides. Geologists study how the Earth formed, what our planet is like, and how it is changing. Geology is one of the earth sciences, or geosciences, that include everything about planet Earth.

ONE DISASTER LEADS TO ANOTHER

Other kinds of disasters often cause mudflows and landslides. Those disasters include hurricanes, earthquakes and volcanic eruptions.

Hurricanes are huge storms that produce heavy rain. The rain soaks the ground and may cause mudflows.

Earthquakes are shaking movements of the ground. Earthquakes can cause landslides. When the ground shakes, loose rocks and soil on top of hills and mountains can tumble down. In 2005 a strong earthquake in Pakistan, a country in southern Asia, caused landslides that killed hundreds of people. 'Whole mountainsides have disappeared,' said Rab Nawaz, who was in Pakistan at the time. 'There is just a big gap where the mountain has slipped into the river.'

A massive earthquake in Pakistan in 2005 caused aftershocks and landslides that killed many people and damaged many roads such as this one.

Volcanoes have caused some of the world's worst mudflows. Soil on the slopes of a volcano is made from volcanic ash and dust. This soil is very fine. When it mixes with water, the soil changes into slippery mud. The mud can flow quickly down the mountainsides. Volcanic mudflows are called lahars.

Volcanoes supply the water that causes lahars. Heat from an eruption can melt snow and ice on the sides of a volcano. An eruption also may release steam or underground pockets of water.

Mudflows from volcanic eruptions may be boiling hot. They can burn people and animals to death. In 1985 more than 23,000 people died in the hot mud flowing from a volcano in the South American country of Colombia.

DID YOU KNOW?

Landslides and mudflows are part of a natural process called erosion. Erosion happens when wind, water and ice slowly wear down mountains and hills.

PEOPLE PLAY A ROLE

Some things that people do can cause mudflows and landslides. People's actions can also make these disasters worse.

Some mudflows and landslides happen because of deforestation (the clearing of trees). People cut down too many trees and other plants on mountains and hillsides. Plants have roots that grow down into the soil. The roots help to hold the soil in place. The leaves and branches of plants also slow down rain as it falls. They act like

Deforestation led to this mudflow in Japan.

In 1982 a lahar flowed down the sides
of Galunggung, a volcano on the island
of Java in Indonesia.

umbrellas. They keep rain from splashing onto the soil and washing it away.

Bare mountainsides and hillsides are disasters waiting to happen. People living in villages around Mount Sarno in Italy cut down trees on the mountainside. They cleared bushes and grass to make fields for farming. In 1998 heavy rains sent rivers of mud roaring down the bare ground. The mudflows killed about 135 people.

RUBBISH SLIDE!

Things that people build can also cause landslides. For years, the city of Manila, in the Philippines in south-eastern Asia, dumped its rubbish in one spot. The pile of rubbish grew into a mountain 20 m high. Hundreds of poor people lived around the pile. They earned money by sorting through the rubbish and selling things that could be recycled.

In 2000, a tall, unstable pile of rubbish mixed with rain fell on the makeshift housing of residents in Quezon City, a suburb of Manila, in the Philippines.

In July 2000, heavy rain soaked the rubbish with water. Part of the mountain of rubbish slid down. 'I was sleeping when I thought I heard an aeroplane coming,' said nine-year-old Nelda Taglo. 'Then there was an explosion. My papa saved me.' The rubbish slide killed at least 200 people. Piles of sand, mining waste and other material can slide in the same way.

Houses, roads, and other structures built in the wrong places also can cause landslides. Soil has to be moved to build these structures. Hills may end up being steeper than they were before. Then the ground is more likely to slip. The weight of these structures also can cause soil and rock to tumble down.

Rivers of mud burst into the town of Sarno in southern Italy in 1998.

'It's the fault of all of us, because we destroyed nature, we burned forests to build houses.'

– Francesco Amato, who carried his family to safety after a mudflow hit Sarno, Italy, in 1998

1966
THE ABERFAN DISASTER

The 1966 landslide devastated t
small Welsh town of Aberfan.

It was a foggy day in Aberfan, in the Merthyr Vale, Wales, on 21 October 1966. At 9.15 am children from the Pantglas Junior School had just finished singing hymns during assembly and were slowly walking out of the assembly hall to return to their classrooms. Suddenly they heard a terrible noise. Seconds later the whole school was engulfed by a giant landslide.

Following a week of heavy rain a huge pile of slag (unwanted rock and mining waste) from a nearby coal mine

Merthyr Mountain. This enormous landslide destroyed 20 houses and a farm before smashing into the school at the bottom on the mountain. Gaynor Minett recalled the event four years later *'It was a tremendous rumbling sound and all the school went dead. You could hear a pin drop. Everyone just froze in their seats. I just managed to get up and I reached the end of my desk when the sound got louder and nearer, until I could see the black out of the*

This was when the landslide hit the primary school. George Williams, who survived the landslide despite being trapped in the wreckage, remembered the deathly quiet after the landslide struck, **'In that silence you couldn't hear a bird or a child'**. Another schoolchild who witnessed the disaster said **'As I was walking up the hill where it turns left, I saw a big wave of muck coming over the railway embankment. It was coming straight towards me and I ran. ... I saw trams, trees, trucks, bricks and boulders in it.'**

Following the tragic event the Aberfan Disaster Fund was set up. The fund generated £1.5 million from over 90,000 contributions within the first four months. A portion of the money was divided among the families of the victims while some of it went towards repairing the damaged houses. As the National Coal Board, the owners of the mine, refused to take financial responsibility for the disaster, money from the fund also had to be used to remove several other slag heaps remaining on the mountainside.

The Aberfan landslide claimed the lives of 144 people, including 116 children and 5 teachers from the Pantglas Junior School. It remains one of the worst man-made disasters in British history.

'I was there for about an hour and a half until the fire brigade found me. I heard cries and screams, but I couldn't move. The desk was jammed into my stomach and my leg was under the radiator.'

– Pupil, Pantglas Junior School, a survivor from the Aberfan landslide of 1966

Mudflow and Landslide Country

LANDSLIDES CAN HAPPEN WHEREVER THERE ARE HIGH PLACES. THE HIGH SPOTS ARE OFTEN NATURAL FORMATIONS — MOUNTAINS, HILLS OR CLIFFS. THEY ALSO MAY BE PILES OF SOIL, RUBBISH OR OTHER MATERIAL BUILT BY PEOPLE.

Mudflows happen in high places where water is present. Mudflows need water to form mud. That water usually comes from rain or melting snow.

LANDSLIDE COUNTRY

Billions of people around the world live in areas affected by landslides and mudflows. Some live near steep mountains, such as Canada's Rocky Mountains.

Landslides and mudflows are especially common in the 'Ring of Fire'. This is a region surrounding the Pacific

SSS SLIDE

One of the most expensive landslides in history happened in Thistle, Utah, USA, in 1983 *(below)*. A wall of soil and rock 300 m wide, 60 m thick and 1.6 km (1 mile) long blocked the Spanish Fork River. The river flooded the town of Thistle. The landslide also blocked a roads and railway lines. It caused about $500 million worth of damage.

Ocean. Most of the world's volcanic eruptions and earthquakes happen there. The ring runs north from Chile along the South American and North American coasts to Alaska. It continues east to Japan and the Philippines and south to New Zealand. Areas that receive very high levels of rainfall are also very susceptible to mudflows or landslides. Landslides in Bangladesh, the Philippines and Venezuela have all been attributed to torrential rain.

Terrible mudflows have happened near volcanoes in the United States, especially Mount Rainier and Mount Saint Helens in Washington State. About 500 years ago, for example, rivers of mud 5 m deep flowed from Mount Rainier. Few people lived nearby when this happened. Since then, however, more people have moved to the area. About 100,000 people live right where the mud could flow.

Thousands of people would be affected if mud flowed down Mount Rainier again.

DISASTER ZONES

Mudflows and landslides happen all around the world. This map shows just a few of the major mudflow and landslide disasters that have taken place over the centuries. The boxed information describes some of the most important disasters.

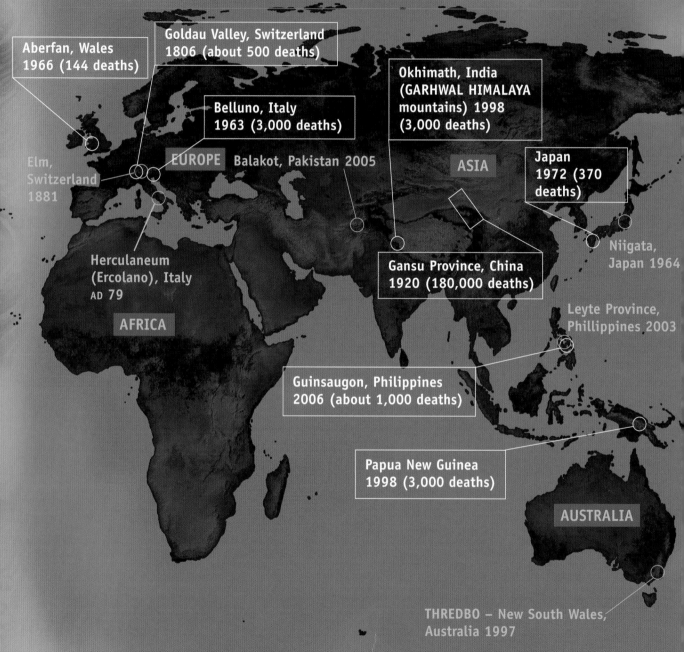

Aberfan, Wales 1966 (144 deaths)

Goldau Valley, Switzerland 1806 (about 500 deaths)

Okhimath, India (GARHWAL HIMALAYA mountains) 1998 (3,000 deaths)

Belluno, Italy 1963 (3,000 deaths)

Elm, Switzerland 1881

EUROPE

Balakot, Pakistan 2005

ASIA

Japan 1972 (370 deaths)

Niigata, Japan 1964

Herculaneum (Ercolano), Italy AD 79

Gansu Province, China 1920 (180,000 deaths)

AFRICA

Leyte Province, Phillippines 2003

Guinsaugon, Philippines 2006 (about 1,000 deaths)

Papua New Guinea 1998 (3,000 deaths)

AUSTRALIA

THREDBO – New South Wales, Australia 1997

TURTLE MOUNTAIN
(Alberta, Canada)
1853 (about 100 deaths)
1903 (70 deaths)

Lituya Bay, AK 1958

Saint-Jean-Vianney
(Quebec, Canada) 1971

MOUNT SAINT HELENS
– Washington 1980

NORTH AMERICA

Thistle,
Utah 1983

Haiti and the
Dominican Republic 2004

La Conchita, California 2005

Mameyes, Puerto Rico
1985 (at least 129
deaths)

Panabaj, Guatemala
2005 (750+ deaths)

Medellín, Colombia
1987 (200 deaths)

Armero, Colombia
1985 (23,000+ deaths)

COTOPAXI VOLCANO – Ecuador 1877

SOUTH AMERICA

MOUNT HUASCARÁN (Peru)
1970 (18,000 deaths)

1980 MOUNT SAINT HELENS

The dark part of Mount Saint Helens is where the lahar flowed during the eruption in 1980.

TV news reporter Dave Crockett was filming a report on Mount Saint Helens, a volcano in Washington State. Suddenly, Crockett felt the ground shake. He heard a rumble. The volcano was erupting.

'I . . . looked in my rearview mirror and there was just a wall of [rock and mud],' he said. *'The whole valley was just disappearing behind me.'*

Crockett almost was buried alive in the biggest landslide and mudflow ever recorded. The disaster started when hot gas from the eruption melted snow and ice on the sides of Mount Saint Helens. About 174 billion litres of hot water rushed down the mountain. The water picked up soil and became a mudflow.

Janet Hicks and her husband watched from a distance as the mudflow carried houses and tractors past their home. Then a big wave of mud carried their house away. **'We were numb and scared,'** said Hicks.

At almost the same time, the eruption blew the top off Mount Saint Helens. The uppermost 400 m of the mountain tumbled down in a landslide. Dorothy and Keith Stoffel were eyewitnesses. These scientists were flying above Mount Saint Helens in an aeroplane. **'Within a matter of seconds, perhaps 15 seconds, the whole north side of the [top] began to move,'** said Keith Stoffel.

The landslide covered an area of 62 square km (24 square miles). It moved more than 21 km (13 miles) down the mountainside into a valley below. At one point, the landslide spilled right over a hill more than 351 m high. It filled parts of the valley to a depth of about 46 m.

Spirit Lake was in the landslide's path. The lake's water is usually cold — about 6°C. When the hot rock and soil fell in, the water temperature rose to 38°C. Rock and mud 90 m deep collected on the lake's bottom.

The mudflows and landslides carried rocks, boulders as big as cars, and whole trees. They destroyed everything in their path, including millions of trees, about 200 homes, 27 bridges, and 300 km (185 miles) of roads. The disaster killed 57 people.

Heavy ash buried this car after the volcano blew.

Measuring Mudflows and Landslides

MEASURING DISASTERS IS IMPORTANT. PEOPLE NEED TO KNOW HOW SERIOUS DISASTERS ARE, AS THIS INFORMATION CAN HELP RESCUE WORKERS DECIDE HOW MUCH HELP TO SEND. SCIENTISTS CAN USE THE INFORMATION TO STUDY DISASTERS. SOMETIMES SCIENTISTS LEARN LESSONS THEY CAN USE TO REDUCE THE DAMAGE FROM FUTURE DISASTERS.

Scientists have developed scales for measuring some kinds of disasters. The Saffir-Simpson scale, for instance, measures the strength of hurricanes. On this scale, a Category 4 hurricane has stronger winds and causes more damage than a Category 1 hurricane. Scientists use the landslide velocity (speed) scale to describe landslides.

PUTTING LANDSLIDES IN CLASSES

The landslide velocity scale was invented in 1996 by David J Varnes and David M Cruden. These geologists put landslides into different classes (groups) numbered from 1 to 7. The classes are based on the speed at which the rock and soil moves and the amount of damage that is caused.

The fastest landslides are Class 7. These landslides travel down at more than 5 m per second and they can cause huge disasters. They can destroy buildings and kill many people. Class 6 landslides cause less damage than Class 7 landslides, but they still kill or injure people who do not have enough time to escape.

The slowest landslides have the lowest numbers on the scale. Class 2 landslides may tilt fences. Over time, they may crack walls or cause other

This landslide at Turtle Mountain in Canada in 1903 was a Class 7 disaster.

LANDSLIDE VELOCITY SCALE

CLASS	DESCRIPTION	SPEED IN CM/DAY	AMOUNT OF DAMAGE
I	EXTREMELY SLOW	< 0.0043	THE MOVEMENT IS SO SLOW THAT IT CAN BE DETECTED ONLY WITH SPECIAL INSTRUMENTS.
2	VERY SLOW	0.0043–0.43	BUILDINGS AND ROADS HAVE ONLY MINOR DAMAGE.
3	SLOW	0.43–43	SOME DAMAGED BUILDINGS CAN BE REPAIRED DURING THE MOVEMENT.
4	MODERATE	43–4,300	ROADS AND STRONG BUILDINGS CAN BE REPAIRED TEMPORARILY DURING THE MOVEMENT.
5	RAPID	4,300–430,000 (43–430 M)	PEOPLE ARE ABLE TO ESCAPE. BUILDINGS ARE DAMAGED.
6	VERY RAPID	430,000–43,000,00 (430 M–43KM)	SOME PEOPLE ARE KILLED. BUILDINGS ARE DESTROYED.
7	EXTREMELY RAPID	> 43,000,000 (> 43KM)	THIS IS A MAJOR DISASTER. PEOPLE HAVE NO TIME TO ESCAPE, SO MANY DIE. BUILDINGS ARE DESTROYED.

damage to buildings. Class 1 landslides move so slowly that they can't be seen. Scientists use instruments to measure these landslides.

DANGER SIGNS

People often see or hear warning signs before major landslides take place. Cracks may open up in the ground. Telegraph poles may start to lean. The warnings give people a chance to evacuate. But the landslide still may damage property.

Slower landslides don't provide as many warning signs. But they may give people enough time to build walls or fences to protect roads or buildings in their path.

SPEED AND SIZE

Speed is very important. A mountainside that breaks off and falls in a split second will cause more damage than a landslide that takes weeks to happen. Fast landslides also injure more people than slow landslides. That's because fast landslides give people little time to escape.

LANDSLIDES YOU'VE SEEN

Have you ever travelled along a road that runs through steep hills? If you have, did you see any rocks along the sides of the road? They probably tumbled down during small landslides. People sometimes build high wire fences along roads that are next to steep cliffs. The fences stop rocks landing on the road and causing car accidents.

The seriousness of a landslide or mudflow also depends on the amount of land that moves. The 1980 landslide at Mount Saint Helens involved 2.8 billion cubic metres of soil and rock. Mount Saint Helens was a much worse disaster than a 2005 mudflow in La Conchita, California, USA. That mudflow involved only 191,000 cubic metres of earth.

WILL LAND SLIDE?

Scientists measure the risk that landslides and mudflows will happen in different places. Knowing the risk is important. If people know a landslide or mudflow is likely, they can prepare for it. They can take steps to limit the amount of damage these events will cause.

In 2005, mud raced down the hillside in La Conchita, giving residents of this California town little time to escape.

People can avoid building homes in areas that have a high risk of landslides. People who already live in a danger zone can stay alert during wet weather or other conditions that can cause a mudflow or landslide. If a landslide begins, they will have a better chance of escaping.

To measure the risk, scientists check the steepness of hills or mountains in areas where people live. They find out how much rain the area gets and the kinds of soil and rock in the ground. Scientists also find out whether earthquakes or volcanic eruptions happen nearby and whether landslides have happened in the past.

QUICK CLAY SLIDES

Some places in Canada, Sweden, Norway and other northern countries have a special kind of clay under the ground. It is called quick clay. It looks like regular clay. Smack a chunk of it, however, and it turns into muddy water. Earthquakes give quick clay that same kind of smack. When the ground shakes, the hard clay under the surface becomes mud. Then the land above the quick clay slides down.

These houses in Gothenburg, Sweden, were built on a clay bed. The clay gave way during a landslide in 1977.

A scientist in the Philippines uses a map to show where landslides are likely to happen.

LISTENING TO ROCKS

Small soil and rock movements often happen before bigger landslides. Scientists use instruments to measure these movements.

Scientists use devices called tiltmeters to measure changes in the tilt (steepness) of mountains and hills. Several tiltmeters may be placed in holes drilled into a mountain. The tiltmeters send signals that show any movement in the mountainside. Any change may mean a landslide is coming.

Other devices show how far the ground has moved. These devices get signals from the Global Positioning Satellite (GPS) system. GPS satellites show the position of every point on the Earth.

Scientists may also listen to rocks. They use microphone-like tools. These tools let them hear sounds that rock makes as it slides.

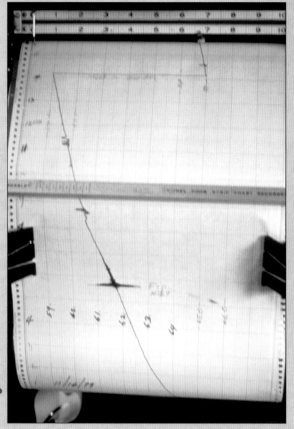

A tiltmeter measures movement of Hawaii's Kilauea Volcano.

A landslide took away the foundations of this house near Wellington, New Zealand, in 2006.

After the eruption of Nevado del Ruiz, a volcano in Colombia, the mixture of ash, ice, and snow created a massive mudflow.

1985
NEVADO DEL RUIZ

On 13 November 1985, geology student Jose Luis Restrepo and his friends were on a university field trip. They had travelled by bus to Armero, Colombia, a city of about 27,000 people. After going out to eat, they went back to their hotel and listened to the radio. At around 11 PM, the radio station suddenly went off the air. A few seconds later, the electricity went off.

'[T]hat's when we started hearing the noise in the air,' said Restrepo, 'like something toppling, falling. . . . Suddenly, I heard bangs and looking towards the rear of the hotel I saw something like foam, coming down out of the darkness. . . . It was a wall of mud approaching the hotel, and sure enough, it crashed against the rear of the hotel and started crushing walls.'

Restrepo and his friends ran for their bus in the hotel car park. They discovered that it **'was higher than us on a wave of mud and on fire.'**

The mudflow had travelled 48 km (30 miles) from the top of the Nevado del Ruiz volcano. Although Colombia's weather is very warm, Nevado del

Rescuers try to pull a body from the mud in Armero.

Ruiz is more than 5,334 m high. At its top, the air is very cold.

Snow about 9 m deep covered the volcano's top. The mountain also had glaciers (sheets of ice) up to 90 m thick. During the eruption, hot gas and melted rock poured out of Nevado del Ruiz. That hot material melted the ice and snow. The water formed one of the world's deadliest mudflows.

Mud poured down the mountain and headed towards Armero. People in the city had no warning. Many were already in bed, sound asleep.

'[The mud] dragged me about 3 km [2 miles],' said Modesto Menesses, a taxi driver in Armero. **'[It] grabbed me and pushed me under. I would come up again and again. I couldn't**

breathe....**The mud was in my nose, mouth and ears.'**

Alba Triviedo heard the mud's roar and took her children outside. **'The mud tore down our house,'** Triviedo said. **'Everything around us was**

"I covered my face, thinking, this is where I die a horrible death."

– Jose Luis Restrepo, describing his experiences during the 1985 Nevado del Ruiz mudflow in Colombia

destroyed, but it didn't touch us. It was a miracle we lived.'

About 23,000 people in Colombia – including 3 out of every 4 people in Armero – were buried alive in the mud. The mudflow injured 4,500 other people. It destroyed much of Armero and a nearby village, including the homes where 8,000 people lived. Repairing the damage cost $1 billion.

People Helping People

PEOPLE NEED HELP AFTER A BIG MUDFLOW OR LANDSLIDE. SOME PEOPLE MAY BE TRAPPED UNDER MUD, STONES OR THE WRECKAGE OF BROKEN BUILDINGS. OTHERS MAY HAVE CUTS OR BROKEN BONES. SOME MAY HAVE LOST THEIR HOMES. THEY MAY HAVE NO CLOTHING, WATER OR FOOD.

Getting help to the victims of mudflows or landslides can be hard. Roads are often blocked and bridges are smashed. Rescue workers may have trouble getting in.

DIFFICULT DISASTERS

When rescue workers do arrive, their work is harder than in some other disasters. After earthquakes, for instance, victims may be trapped under broken buildings. After mudflows and landslides, people may be trapped under buildings that are covered with mud, earth or rocks.

'You can see only the roofs of a few houses,' said a rescue official at a landslide in Medellín, Colombia. The workers tried to dig through dirt 11 m deep with shovels, sticks and even their bare hands.

MUDDY MYSTERY

A woman looked out of her window one night in 1971 and was amazed to see lights from the next village. A hill had always blocked that view. She called a friend and they discussed what might have happened to the hill. They didn't know that heavy rain had turned that hill into a 20 m-high river of mud. It was rushing towards the woman's house in Saint-Jean-Vianney, Quebec, Canada. The mudflow swept the woman away, along with a bridge, a bus, 40 houses and 30 other people.

Rocks blocked the roads to hard-to-reach villages after an earthquake shook northern Pakistan in 2005.

Fast action is important in these disasters. People buried in mud cannot breathe. Without air, they can live for only a few minutes. But some lucky ones are buried in places where air is trapped in pockets (holes). They can sometimes live for days while waiting for help.

THE NOSE KNOWS

In developing countries, rescue workers often use poles to search for victims buried by mudflows or landslides. Workers gently push the poles into the dirt, hoping to feel when the poles touch a body. Then they move a few steps ahead and push again.

Rescue workers in developed countries have more advanced ways of searching for victims. These workers often use rescue dogs. Dogs can smell and hear much better than people. Rescue dogs are trained to use their noses and ears to find victims. When a dog finds a person, rescue workers can dig quickly and free the person.

In the 2005 mudflow in La Conchita, California, rescuers lowered microphones into holes in the wreckage. The microphones were powerful enough to pick up moans, breathing and other sounds made by people buried underneath the surface.

CADAVER DOGS

Search and rescue teams try to find living disaster victims, but they also look for people who have died. These teams use cadaver dogs, which are trained to find the scent of cadavers (dead human bodies). Finding these bodies is very important. When a victim's body is found, the victim's family and friends can accept that the person really is dead. They can express grief over their loss and say goodbye to their loved one.

WHAT A RELIEF!

While rescue workers search for survivors, the other victims need relief. They need help to reduce their suffering. 'What we need most is medicine, mattresses, blankets and jackets,' said Diego Esquina. He was the mayor of Panabaj, Guatemala, when it was hit by a mudflow in 2005.

Boonie, a cadaver dog, searches for bodies following a deadly landslide in La Conchita, California, in 2005.

Medicine and household items aren't all that victims of mudflows and landslides need. Some of them may have lost everything they own. Their homes may be so badly damaged that it is unsafe to go back inside. These people need a new place to live.

People are often evacuated to another area, away from the disaster. At first, they may live in tents or in shelters. Schools or other buildings are used as temporary shelters. They have beds and food for people who have been evacuated.

DISASTER RELIEF WORKERS

IThe first help in a disaster usually comes from local fire brigades and police. They arrive at the scene quickly start to work. In big disasters, soldiers from the army also help. They provide water, food, clothing and places for people to live.

People from around the country often give money to help the victims. Shops and other businesses may send water, clothing and other products.

MANY HELPING HANDS

In other countries, some help comes from the International Federation of Red Cross and Red Crescent Societies. This is the world's biggest private organization that helps in disasters. Red Cross and Red Crescent workers stay for months to help people rebuild their lives. Almost all countries have a Red Cross or Red Crescent organization. When a disaster strikes, people from around the world help by sending money to those organizations.

The United Nations, a group of more than 190 countries, also provides relief after disasters. The governments of countries around the world send workers and money.

DISASTER RELIEF KITS

The first help for survivors often comes in kits that relief workers pass out. Water is one of the most important items in these kits. Mudflows and landslides can break pipes that carry drinking water. They also can pollute wells, rivers and lakes where people get water to drink.

Polluted water contains germs. If people drink it, they can become very sick. Some people who survive a disaster die because they had to drink polluted water.

Soldiers unload relief supplies after a mudflow cut off villages in the north-eastern Philippines in 2004.

Relief kits contain a few bottles of water to keep people healthy until trucks and aeroplanes can bring in much more. The kits also contain food, blankets, soap and other essential items.

GETTING A LIFE BACK

After the relief efforts end, disaster victims need help to recover. They need help getting their lives back to normal. Even after terrible disasters, people do spring back. They rebuild roads, bridges and even entire cities. Schools, shops and cinemas open again. People go back to work and live normally.

Rebuilding lives can take a long time. That's especially true in developing countries, where the governments cannot afford to provide much help to their people. In these countries, some of the money for rebuilding comes from the same organizations that provided disaster relief.

In the UK, many people have insurance for their homes and cars. People with insurance pay small amounts of money to insurance companies. Then, if a disaster strikes, the insurance company provides the money to replace or repair damaged items.

Recovery may mean moving out of harm's way. Mudflows and landslides often happen over and over again in the same areas. In some countries government agencies buy the homes of people who live in these areas. The people use the money to move to a safer place. Then they will not become disaster victims again.

This shopkeeper is removing mud from the entrance to his business in Infanta, the Philippines, December 2004.

"We have nothing left. Everything is destroyed. We didn't even manage to save our clothes."

– Celia Huerto, whose family survived a series of tropical storms and mudflows in the Philippines in 2004

A photo taken from the air shows the devastation caused by the mudflow in La Conchita.

2005
LA CONCHITA, CALIFORNIA, USA

Rain soaked La Conchita, California, USA. This town of 240 people had had almost as much rain in two weeks as it usually receives in a year. La Conchita is located on a narrow strip of land. The Pacific Ocean is on one side. Steep hills about 180 m high are on the other.

People were worried about the hills. After heavy rain in 1995, the hills had slid into La Conchita, burying houses under 540,000 tonnes of mud. *'We knew the mountain was coming down [again],'* said Greg Ray, who lived in the town. But nobody knew when.

After the 1995 mudflow, the local council put up signs outside La Conchita. They warned, 'Enter at Your Own Risk.' But people took the signs down. *'Everyone got used to [the risk of another mudflow],'* said Gisela Woggon, another resident. *'People started moving back, even moving into houses at the edge of the old* slide.'

Around 12.30 PM on 10 January 2005, the hills slid into La Conchita again. Ray and his friend Tony Alvis were helping a neighbour move out of a house below a steep hill. *[John Morgan, another neighbour,] yelled at us and said, 'The mountain's coming down – get out of there now!'*

They ran for their lives as 360,000 tonnes of mud and rocks rushed down. Ray could hear the roar of the mud as he ran. Out of the corner of one eye, he saw that the river of mud was carrying a house and a caravan, and it was catching up with him.

Ray dived between two parked cars just as the mud and wreckage slopped down. His quick thinking saved him.

Wet, thick mud trapped trucks along Highway 101, a major freeway near La Conchita.

Morgan and Alvis were not so lucky. Both men died when the mudflow pulled them under.

Resident Jimmie Wallet's wife and three daughters died because there was no warning. 'They never had a chance to get out,' said Scott Hall, a firefighter who was at the disaster. 'It appeared they were sitting on a couch unaware of the slide.'

Mud 10 m deep buried part of La Conchita. It killed 10 people and seriously injured 8 others. The mudflow destroyed about 13 houses. Some were carried away and stacked up, one against another. More than 20 other homes were badly damaged.

' I thought I was going to die buried alive.... The house started collapsing on me. ...I could feel the boards and the rocks and everything pushing me. '

– Diane Hart, describing the 2005 mudflow in La Conchita, California

49

The Future

WE HAVE LEARNED LESSONS FROM PAST MUDFLOWS AND LANDSLIDES. THOSE LESSONS WILL HELP TO MAKE LIFE SAFER FOR PEOPLE IN THE FUTURE. MANY PEOPLE WHO HAVE DIED IN MUDFLOWS AND LANDSLIDES COULD HAVE BEEN SAVED. THEY JUST NEEDED A WARNING THAT THE MUD WAS ON ITS WAY.

Safety was just a few minutes' walk away for many of the 23,000 people who died in mudflows from the Nevado del Ruiz volcano in 1985. What if sirens had warned them? The mud flowed in a fairly narrow path through the town of Armero. People could have walked a short distance to safety. Instead, the mud swallowed them alive.

LISTENING FOR MUD

Scientists have invented warning systems for mudflows and avalanches. Acoustic flow monitors (AFMs) are used in mudflow warning systems. These devices measure sounds that occur in the ground as mud flows. They can also estimate the size of the flow.

This acoustic flow monitor keeps an ear out for mud flowing in Hoala, Hawaii.

When AFMs detect a mudflow, they send a signal to a control centre. The centre then alerts fire stations, police and emergency workers. Warnings go out via radio, television and the Internet.

AFM systems have already been installed on a few volcanoes where mudflows pose a great danger. In the US, Mount Saint Helens and Mount Rainier in Washington State and the Hoala Volcano in Hawaii have these systems. Scientists plan to put AFMs and other warning systems in more places where mudflows and landslides are a danger.

A bulldozer repairs damage from a
2006 landslide in Provo, Utah, USA.

MORE AND BETTER WARNINGS

In the future, more people in these danger zones will know how to use the warnings. Communities will have evacuation plans that tell people what to do and where to go when a disaster threatens.

Future warning systems will be more accurate. All too often, warning devices give false alarms. They sometimes send warnings when there is no real danger.

False alarms can be dangerous. People may be injured or killed as they rush to evacuate a danger zone. Also what happens if there are too many false alarms? People may ignore the warning when a real disaster is on the way.

OPEN your EYES!

Scientists and emergency workers are looking for better ways to make people aware of the risk of disasters. Telling people about the risk is especially important for mudflows and landslides. That's because these disasters often happen again and again in the same places.

Why do people keep living in disaster zones? Why do they build new homes, schools and shops in places where there are disasters waiting to happen? Getting people to live in safer areas could mean a future in which fewer people are hurt by landslides and mudflows.

BETTER EYES IN THE SKY

Scientists are building better cameras and other instruments that will detect landslides and mudflows from satellites in space. These instruments will map landslide and mudflow danger zones all over the Earth.

Cameras that provide sharper pictures are important. They will allow scientists to make better maps of areas where disasters have

This sign in south-western Germany warns people that landslides can happen in the area.

Mud and debris swirl around a building at the foot of El Salvador's Ilamatepec volcano. About 10,000 Salvadorans lived near the volcano when it erupted in 2005.

happened in the past. People who live in these areas then will know that they face a similar danger.

Other instruments may allow scientists to watch for tiny movements in mountains and hills. If a hillside slides 2.5 cm today and 30 cm tomorrow, it may be getting ready for a disastrous landslide.

REDUCING THE DANGER

Such information will help people reduce the damage from mudflows and landslides in the future. People can move away from danger zones. They can install warning systems, plant trees on slopes to hold the soil in place and plan for evacuations.

Mudflows and landslides are dangerous, but they also are rare. They happen mainly in places near mountains, hills or high piles of soil or other material. With better warnings and information on mudflow and landslide safety, most people can avoid these disasters.

Cracks in the ground near the city of Skopje, Macedonia, where a landslide happened in 2006.

PREPARING FOR LANDSLIDES AND MUDFLOWS

Landslides and mudflows usually strike with little or no warning. It is important to know the danger signs and what to do to protect yourself and your family. Warning signs can include:

- New cracks or unusual bulges in the ground, street or pavements

- Sudden tilting of trees, fences, telegraph poles or street signs

- Doors or windows that stick for the first time

If a mudflow or landslide is on the way, you may hear a rumbling or rushing sound. You may see a river of mud or tumbling rock and soil. If you do, remember to:

- Run to the side, in a direction away from the danger.

- If possible, head for a hill or other high ground. Try to find shelter, such as a group of trees or a strong building.

- If you cannot escape a landslide, curl into a tight ball and protect your head.

- If you are caught in a mudflow, grab onto a tree or other object that is being carried along.

After a mudflow or landslide:

- Stay away from the area. More mud or rocks may be on the way. Wait until emergency officials say it is safe to return.

- Don't go into damaged buildings. They may fall down and trap you. Cracks in a chimney or foundation can mean that a house is badly damaged.

- Stay away from electrical power lines and telephone lines that may have fallen down. The electricity could hurt you.

Timeline

AD 79 Mud from the eruption of Mount Vesuvius *(right)* in modern-day Italy buries the city of Herculaneum.

1806 Part of Rossberg Peak in Switzerland collapses and kills 500 people.

1853 A landslide on Turtle Mountain, Alberta, Canada, kills over 100 people.

1877 One mudflow in Ecuador travels more than 320 km (192 miles).

1881 A mountaintop near Elm, Switzerland, weakened by slate mining, collapses. More than 7.5 million cubic m of rock hurtles down the mountain and devastates the towns below.

1903 Coal mining weakens Turtle Mountain in Alberta, Canada and 82 million tonnes of rock cascade on the town of Frank. The landslide kills at least 70 people.

1920 An earthquake causes a huge landslide in Gansu Province, China, killing approximately 180,000 people.

1958 A landslide in Lituya Bay, Alaska, generates a tsunami wave over 15 m high.

1963 A landslide into the Vaiont Dam in Belluno, Italy, causes a huge wave 100 m high to wash over the dam and kill 3,000 people in the village of Longarone.

1964 44,000 people are left homeless after a landslide destroys bridges and homes in Niigata, Japan.

1966 A slag pile (unwanted rock from coal mines) in Aberfan, Wales *(left)*, collapses and slams into a school, killing 144 people.

1970 A magnitude 7.9 earthquake in the central mountains of Peru creates a landslide that kills approximately 66,000 people.

1971 A 20-m river of mud buries the town of Saint-Jean-Vianney in Canada.

1972 Floods in Japan cause a landslide that kills 370 people and causes a $472 million loss of crops and homes.

1980 Mount Saint Helens erupts and destroys more than 600 sq km (230 square miles) of land.

1983 The most expensive landslide in the United States buries Thistle, Utah. The damage totals approximately $500 million.

1985 23,000 people are killed when mud from the slopes of the Nevado del Ruiz volcano buries the town of Armero, Colombia *(right)*.

1998 Deforestation in the Himalayan mountains and torrential rains are blamed for a massive series of landslides in India.

2000 A rain-soaked mountain of rubbish crashes into makeshift housing in Quezon City, the Philippines. More than 100 people are killed.

2002 A landslide that was 20 miles (30 km) long fills the Karmadon Gorge *(below)* with rock and mud. The disaster completely covers the village of Nizhny Karmadon in southern Russia.

2004 The island of Hispaniola is devastated by flooding as high as 4.6 m that sends rivers of mud down to the villages below.

2005 Mudflows in Mexico and Central America, caused by Hurricane Stan, kill at least 750 people, injure hundreds of others and destroy the homes where about 100,000 people live.

2006 Heavy rains and a minor earthquake cause a series of deadly mudflows in southern Leyte Province in the Philippines.

Glossary

ash: tiny bits of rock that come out of a volcano

creep: a very slow movement of the ground

deforestation: cutting down all the trees and other plants in an area

evacuate: to leave an area for a safer place

friction: the force that makes it harder for one object to slide against another

geologists: scientists who study how the Earth formed, what our planet is like and how it is changing

hurricane: a huge storm with strong, swirling winds that produces heavy rain

inertia: the tendency of still objects to stay still and of objects in motion to stay in motion

lahar: a mudflow that occurs on a volcano

landslide: a mass of soil and rock that breaks loose from a hill or mountain and slides downwards

mudflow: wet earth that flows like a river down the sides of a mountain or hill

slump: soil, rock or other material that drops downwards a short distance onto flat land, then piles up and stops

suffocate: die from lack of air to breathe

tsunami: a wave produced by Earth movement, a volcano or a landslide

volcano: an opening in Earth's surface that sometimes erupts

Place to Visit

The Science Museum London
http://www.sciencemuseum.org.uk
At the science museum in London you can look at the different instruments that have been used to predict measure and record extreme weather.

Source Notes

4 Juan Tacaxoy, quoted in Karin Gezelius Bergstresser, 'Santiago Atitlan, 5 October 2005 Mudslide,' *Santiago Atitlan*, n.d., http://www.santiagoatitlan.com/disaster/disaster1e.html (17 October 2006).

4 Dr. Francisco Mendes Beauc, quoted in Laura Smith-Spark, 'Buried Alive in a River of Mud,' *BBC News*, 10 October 2005, http://news.bbc.co.uk/go/pr/fr/-/1/hi/americas/4326650.stm (10 October 2005).

5 Alexander Flores, quoted in 'Rescuers Struggle in Wake of Stan,' *BBC News*, 6 October 2005, http://news.bbc.co.uk/go/pr/fr/-/1/hi/world/americas/4314088.stm (10 October 2005).

5 Diego Esquina, quoted in 'Guatemala Villages 'Mass Graves,'' *BBC News*, 10 October 2005, http://news.bbc.co.uk/go/pr/fr/-/1/hi/world/americas/4324038.stm (27 November 2005).

5 Alexander Flores, quoted in 'Flooding, Landslide Kill Scores,' *Taipei Times*, 7 October 2005, http://www.taipeitimes.com/News/world/archives/2005/10/07/2003274789 (17 October 2006).

13 Pliny the Younger, quoted in 'Mount Vesuvius,' *Classroom of the Future*, http://www.cet.edu/ete/modules/volcanoes/vmtvesuvius.html (17 October 2006).

13 Ibid.

13 Ibid.

16 Tom Horning, quoted in Jen Shaffer, 'The Science of Slides: A Primer on How Debris Flows Work,' *Wildfire News*, http://www.wildfirenews.com/ forests/forest/analysis.html (3 December 2005).

16–17 Rab Nawaz, quoted in 'Survivors Ponder Life without Livelihoods,' *BBC News*, 29 October 2005, http://news.bbc.co.uk/2/hi/south_asia/4385216.stm (17 October 2006).

20 Nelda Taglo, quoted in Angela Pagano, ''Promised Land' Garbage Landslide Kills at Least 200 in the Philippines,' *World Socialist Web Site*, 21 July 2000, http://www.wsws.org/articles/2000/jul2000/phil-j21_prn.shtml (19 November 2005).

21 Francesco Amato, quoted in Vania Grandi, 'Body Search Continues in Muddy Central Italy,' *Laredo Morning Times*, 8 May 1998, http://www.lmtonline.com/news/archive/050898/pagea13.pdf (16 October 2006).

22 Jessie Byran Leitch, quoted in 'Frank Slide,' *Winnipeg Free Press*, 15 October 1950, http://www.shirley.collongridge.com/FrankSlide02.htm (27 November 2005).

23 Ibid.

28 Dave Crockett, quoted in Jason Manning, '22. Mount St. Helens,' *The Eighties Club*, n.d., http://eightiesclub.tripod.com/id308.htm (17 October 2006).

28 Janet Hicks, quoted in Sally Ousley, 'Eruption Survivors Excited, Nervous,' *Daily News*, 1 October 2004, http://www.tdn.com/helens/noFlash/mainpage.php?p=1114797670&w=P (17 October 2006 2006).

29 Keith Stoffel, quoted in 'Debris Avalanche,' *USGS*, 19 March 2002, http://pubs.usgs.gov/gip/msh//debris.html (17 October 2006).

29 Ibid.

38 Jose Luis Restrepo, quoted in Dr. Vic Camp, 'Nevado del Ruiz (1985),' *How Volcanoes Work*, 10 Oc-tober 2000, http://www.geology.sdsu.edu/how _volcanoes_work/Nevado.html (19 November 2005).

38 Ibid.

39 Modesto Bocanegra Menesses, quoted in Tomas Guillen, 'A Volcano's Toll: Disaster in Colombia,' *Reporter*, n.d., http://fac-staff.seattleu.edu/tomasg/ web/reporter/volcano.html (19 November 2005).

39 Alba Maria Triviedo, quoted in Tomas Guillen, 'A Volcano's Toll: Disaster in Colombia,' *Reporter*, n.d., http://fac-staff.seattleu.edu/tomasg/web/ reporter/volcano.html (19 November 2005).

39 Jose Luis Restrepo.

40 Civil defense official, quoted in Reuters, 'Rescuers Dig for Landslide Victims,' *Chicago Tribune*, 29 November 1987.

42 Diego Esquina, quoted in Frank Jack Daniel, 'Guatemalan Village Turns into 'Cemetery' under Mud,' *Globeandmail.com*, 10 October 2005, http://www.theglobeandmail.com/servlet/story/LAC. 20051010.GUATEMALA10/ (10 October 2005).

47 Celia Huerto, quoted in Mona Laczo, 'Philippines Struggles with Storm Damage,' *BBC News*, 7 December 2004, http://news.bbc.co.uk/ 2/hi/asia-pacific/4074859.stm (18 October 2006).

48 Greg Ray, quoted in Robert Jablon, 'Mudslide Survivor Recalls Horror,' *SouthCoastToday.com*, 14 January 2005, http://www.southcoasttoday .com/daily/01-05/01-14-05/a10lo518.htm (17 November 2005).

48 Gisela Woggon, quoted in 'Southland's Record Rainfall,' *Los Angeles Times*, 12 January 2005.

49 Greg Ray.

49 Scott Hall, quoted in 'Hunt for Mudslide Survivors Ends,' *CBS News*, 13 January 2005, http://www.cbsnews.com/stories/2005/01/14/ national/main666949.shtml (7 October 2005).

49 Diane Hart, quoted in 'Hunt for Mudslide Survivors Ends,' *CBS News*, 13 January 2005, http://www.cbsnews.com/stories/2005/01/14/ national/main666949.shtml (7 October 2005).

Selected Bibliography

American National Red Cross. 'Volcano.' *American Red Cross*. N.d. http://www.redcross.org/services/ disaster/0,1082,0_593_00.html (October 11, 2006).

Bruce, Victoria. *No Apparent Danger: The True Story of Volcanic Disaster at Galeras and Nevado del Ruiz*. New York: HarperCollins, 2001.

College of the Siskiyous. 'Mudflows of Mount Shasta.' *Mount Shasta*. N.d. http://www.siskiyous.edu/ shasta/env/glacial/mud.htm (October 11, 2006).

Davis, Lee. *Natural Disasters*. New York: Facts on File, 2002.

Engelbert, Phillis. *Dangerous Planet: The Science of Natural Disasters*. Detroit: UXL, 2001.

Federal Emergency Management Agency. 'Landslide and Debris Flow (Mudslide).' *FEMA*. March 29, 2006. http://www.fema.gov/hazard/landslide/index.shtm (October 11, 2006).

Gregory, Kenneth John, ed. *The Earth's Natural Forces*. New York: Oxford University Press, 1990.

Hancock, Paul L., and Brian J. Skinner, eds. *Oxford Companion to the Earth*. New York: Oxford University Press, 2000.

Reice, Seth. R. *The Silver Lining: The Benefits of Natural Disasters*. Princeton, NJ: Princeton University Press, 2001.

Spignesi, Stephen J. *The 100 Greatest Disasters of All Time*. New York: Kensington Publishing Corp., 2002.

U.S. Department of the Interior. 'Deadly Lahars from Nevado del Ruiz, Colombia.' *U.S. Geological Survey*. September 30, 1999. http://volcanoes.usgs.gov/Hazards/What/Lahars/RuizLahars.html (October 11, 2006).

——.'FAQs (Frequently Asked Questions).' *U.S. Geological Survey*. November 2, 2005. http://landslides.usgs.gov/learningeducation/faq.php (October 11, 2006).

——.'Mudflows, Debris Flows, and Lahars.' *U.S. Geological Survey*. March 3, 2006. http://vulcan.wr.usgs.gov/Glossary/Lahars/framework.html (October 11, 2006).

Wheeling Jesuit University. 'Mount Ranier.' *Classroom of the Future*. November 10, 2004. http://www.cotf.edu/ete/modules/volcanoes/mountrainier.html (October 11, 2006).

Zeilinga de Boer, Jelle, and Donald Theodore Sanders. *Earthquakes in Human History: The Far Reaching Effects of Seismic Disruptions*. Princeton, NJ: Princeton University Press, 2005.

Further Resources

BOOKS

Baldwin, Carol. *Shaky Ground: Earthquakes* (Turbulent Planet), Raintree Publishers, 2005.

Chancellor, Deborah. *Planet Earth* (Kingfisher Young Knowledge) Kingfisher Books Ltd, 2006

Climate Change (Eyewitness) Dorling Kindersley Publishers Limited, 2008.

Climate Change (Planet Under Pressure) Raintree Publishers, 2007.

Colson, Mary. *Crumbling Earth: Erosion and Landslides* (Turbulent Planet) Raintree Publishers, 2005

Deary, Terry. *Terry Deary's Terribly True Disaster Stories* (Terry Deary's Terribly True Stories) Scholastic, 2006.

Ganeri, Anita. *Earth Shattering Earthquakes and Violent Volcanoes* (Horrible Geography) Scholastic, 2006.

Ganeri, Anita. *Stormy Weather* (Horrible Geography) Scholastic, 2008.

Griffey, Harriet. *Volcanoes and Other Natural Disasters* Dorling Kindersley Publishers Ltd,

Langley, Andrew. *Natural Disasters* (Kingfisher Knowledge) Kingfisher Books, Ltd., 2006.

Senior, Kathryn. *Planet Earth* (Fast Forward) Franklin Watts Ltd, 2000.

Spilsbury, Richard and Louise Spilbury. *Landslides and Avalanches* (Natural Disasters) Wayland, 2007.

61

Spilsbury, Richard and Louise Spilbury. *Thundering Landslides* (Awesome Forces of Nature) Heinemann, 2005.

Van Rose, Susanna. *Volcanoes and Earthquakes* (Eyewitness) Dorling Kindersley Publishers Limited, 2004.

Walker, Sally M. *Earthquakes* (Early Bird Earth Science), Lerner Books, 2009.

Watts, Claire. *Natural Disasters* (Eyewitness) Dorling Kindersley Publishers Limited, 2006.

Weather (Eyewitness) Dorling Kindersley Publishers Ltd, 2006.

Wild Weather (Go Facts: Natural Disasters) A & C Black Limited, 2007.

WEBSITES

BBC – Animated Guide to Volcanoes
http://news.bbc.co.uk/1/hi/sci/tech/4972366.stm
This animation shows how and why a volcano erupts and will help you to explore some of the Earth's major volcanoes.

CBBC Newsround – Volcanoes
http://news.bbc.co.uk/cbbcnews/hi/find_out/guides/tech/volcanoes/newsid_1768000/1768595.stm
Use this website to find out more about volcanoes and to learn some interesting facts.

Natural History Museum – Natural Disasters
http://www.nhm.ac.uk/nature-online/earth/volcanoes-earthquakes/index.html
Find out about the different kinds of natural disasters that affect the Earth. This website includes a section about volcanoes and a video of a volcanic eruption.

The Science Museum – Climate Change
http://www.sciencemuseum.org.uk/antenna/climatechange/
On this website you can learn about the different things that cause climate change, find out how it is measured and read about the consequences it is having. You can also learn about ways in which you can help to stop climate change.

Index

Aberfan 22–23
acoustic flow monitors 50
Armero, Colombia 38, 39, 50

California 11, 33, 42, 43, 48, 49
Canada 16, 34, 40

Central America 4, 5
Colombia 18, 38, 39
creep 8
Cruden, David M 30

deforestation 18, 20

disaster kits 46
disaster zones 26–27, 52, 54
earthquakes. *See* landslides: and earthquakes; mudflows: and earthquakes
El Salvador 4, 5, 53
erosion 18

warnings of 52, 54

evacuations 32, 44, 46, 62

friction 14, 16

geologists 16, 30, 34, 35
gravity 14
Guatemala 4, 5, 42

Hawaii 24, 36, 50
heavy mud 14, 15, 49
Herculaneum, Italy 12–13
hot mud. See lahars
hurricanes 4, 5, 30
Hurricane Stan 4, 5

Ilamatepec Volcano 5, 53
Indonesia 15, 19
inertia 14
Italy 8, 20, 21

Japan 18, 25

Kilauea Volcano 36

La Conchita, California 32, 33, 42,
    43, 44, 48–49
lahars 5, 18, 19, 28
landslides: classes of 30–31; deaths
    by 20, 23; definition of 6; de-
    struction by 6, 8, 10, 20,
    22–23, 24, 29, 30, 31, 32, 34,
    51; and earthquakes 16, 17, 35;
    and human actions 20, 22-23,
    34; makeup of 6, 8; measuring
    30, 31, 36, 52, 54; and moun-
    tains 11, 18, 24, 25, 54; and
    personal stories 16, 18, 20, 29,
    40; and rain 20; signs of 32,
    52, 54, 55; size of 8; study of
    30, 50, 52, 54; and tsunamis
    10; and volcanoes 28–29;

Macedonia 54
Mexico 4, 9
mining 22-23
Mount Rainier 25, 50
Mount Saint Helens 25, 28–29, 32,
    50
Mount Sarno 20, 21
Mount Vesuvius 12, 13
mudflows: causes of 14; deaths by 4,
    5, 9, 13, 18, 20, 39, 49; defini-
    tion of 6; destruction by 4, 7, 8,
    9, 10, 13, 28, 48, 49; and earth-
    quakes 25; and human
    actions 18, 20, 21; and hurri-
    canes 4, 5, 17; makeup of 6, 14,
    16; and mountains 24, 25, 54;
    personal stories of 4, 5, 12–13,
    28, 38–39, 40, 48–49; and rain
    4, 9, 16, 18, 20, 21, 24, 48, 49;
    and rescue work 5; signs of 32,
    52, 54, 55; size of 6; study of
    13, 14, 16, 30, 32, 34, 50, 52,
    54; and volcanoes 5, 12, 14, 16,
    18, 19, 25, 28–29, 38, 39, 50,
    53; warnings of 52

National Coal Board 23
National Guard 44
Nevado del Ruiz 38–39
New Zealand 25, 37
Norway 34

Pakistan 16, 17, 41
Panabaj, Guatemala 4, 5, 42
Papua New Guinea 10
Philippines 20, 25, 35, 45, 47

Red Crescent 44
Red Cross 44
rescue dogs 42, 43
rescue workers 40, 42, 43, 44, 45

Ring of Fire 25
road closures 7, 11, 49

slag heaps 22-23
slumps 6
Sweden 34

Thistle, Utah 24
tsunamis. See landslides: and
    tsunamis

United Nations 44
United States 10, 24, 25, 42, 44,
    46, 50, 51
US Army 44
Utah 51

Varnes, David J 30
volcanoes. See Ilamatepec Volcano;
    Kilauea Volcano; landslides: and
    volcanoes; Mount Rainier;
    Mount Saint Helens; Mount
    Sarno; mudflows: and volca-
    noes; Nevado del Ruiz

Wales 22-23

Photo Acknowledgements

The images in this book are used with the permission of: © Anatoly Maltsev/epa/CORBIS, pp 1, 57 (bottom); © Photodisc/Getty Images, p 1 (background); © ROMEO GACAD/AFP/Getty Images, pp 3, 45, 47, 55; © ORLANDO SIERRA/AFP/Getty Images, p 4; © YURI CORTEZ/AFP/Getty Images, pp 5, 53; © E R Degginger/Photo Researchers, Inc., p 6; © Brian P Biller/US Navy via Getty Images, p 7; © AGRfoto/Alex Rowbotham/Alamy, p 8; © Reuters/CORBIS, p 9; AP Photo/Brian Cassey, p 10; © Tom Myers/Photo Researchers, Inc, p 11; © Mimmo Jodice/CORBIS, p 12; © Atlantide Phototravel/CORBIS, p 13; © BAY ISMOYO/AFP/Getty Images, p 15; © Picture Contact/Alamy, p 17; © Daniel and Flossie White/Alamy, p 18; © Fletcher & Baylis/Photo Researchers, Inc, p 19; AP Photo/Pat Roque, p 20; AP Photo/Franco Castano, p 21; © Fox Photos/Hulton Archive/Getty Images, pp 22, 56 (top); © The Merthyr Express, p 23; Photograph courtesy of Utah Geological Survey, p 24; US Geological Survey, pp 25 (Lyn Topinka), 28 (Tom Casadevall), 29 (Dan Dzurisin), 50 (Tom Hale); George S Rice/Library and Archives Canada, p 31 (PA-045409); AP Photo/Kevork Djansezian, pp 33, 48, 49; © Keystone/Hulton Archive/Getty Images, p 34; © RICO GONZALES/AFP/Getty Images, p 35; © CORBIS, p 36; © Marty Melville/Getty Images, p 37; AP Photo/Paul Benoit, p 38; AP Photo/Carlos Gonzalez, p 39; © TOSHIFUMI KITAMURA/AFP/Getty Images, p 41; AP Photo/Reed Saxon, p 43; AP Photo/George Frey, p 51; © Sigrid Dauth/Alamy, p 52; © ROBERT ATANASOVSKI/AFP/Getty Images, p 54; Library of Congress (LC-DIG-ppmsc-06584), p 56 (bottom); AP Photo, p 57 (top).

Front cover: © Steven Georges/Press-Telegram/CORBIS; © Photodisc/Getty Images (background).

Back cover: © Photodisc/Getty Images.

About the Authors

Michael Woods is a science and medical journalist in Washington, DC, USA, who has won many national writing awards. Mary B Woods is a school librarian. Their past books include the eight-volume Ancient Technology series. Michael and Mary have four children. When not writing, reading or spending time with their grandchildren, they travel to gather material for future books.